كل شيئ ينام
Everything Sleeps

Bilingual Arabic-English Edition

تَرجَمَة هاني الأغبَري
Translation by Hani Alaġbary

رسوم هناء الأغبري
Illustrated by Hana Alaġbary

كتابة اِمى الأغبري
Written by Emma Alaġbary

Words Copyright © 2022 Emma Alaġbary
Illustrations Copyright © 2022 Hana Alaġbary
Translation Copyright © 2022 Hani Alaġbary

All rights reserved. This book or any portion thereof may not be reproduced or used in any manner without the express written permission of the copyright holder.

Published by Little Dragon Books

Dunedin, New Zealand

Bilingual Arabic-English - First Edition
Paperback

ISBN-13: 978-0-473-61847-6

littledragonbooks.com

كل شيئ ينام
Everything Sleeps

Bilingual Arabic-English Edition

السمك ينام و عيناه مفتوحة

Fish sleep with their eyes open.

الأحصنة تنام مستقيمة!

Horses sleep standing up!

الخفاش ينام معلقًا على رجليه

Bats sleep upside down.

ثعلَب الماء ينام متماسك الأيدي

Otters hold hands while they sleep.

الزراف يغفى و رأسه على ظهرة

Giraffes take naps with their
heads on their backs.

الدولفين ينام بعين واحدة مفتوحة

Dolphins sleep with one eye open.

طائر القطرس يأخذ غفوات قصيرة... و هو يطير!

Albatrosses take lots of tiny naps...
while flying!

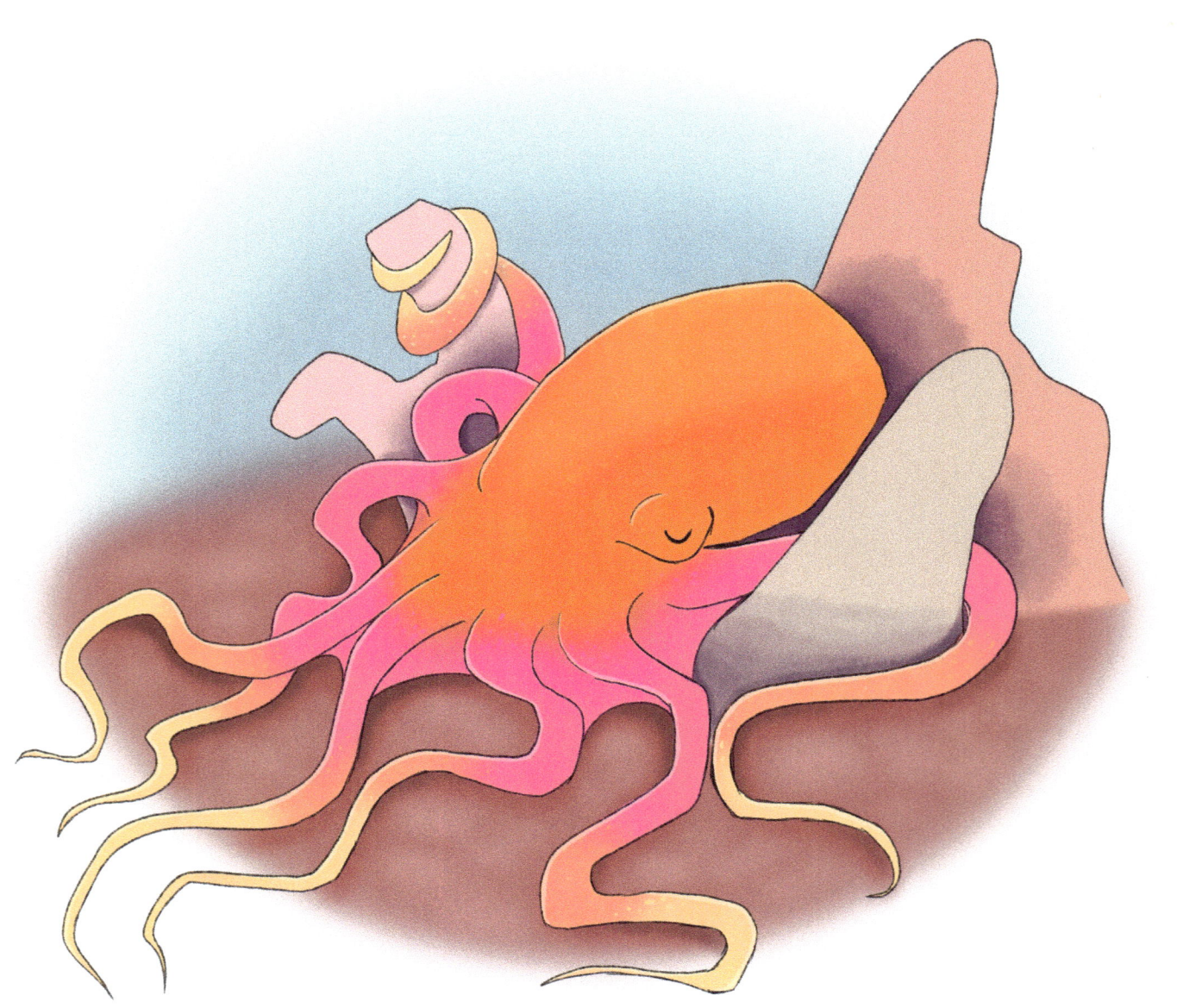

الأخطبوط يغير لونة و هو نائم

Octopi change color while they sleep.

البط تنام بطوابير

Ducks sleep in rows.

السرقاط ينام بالأكوام

Meerkats sleep in piles.

الدب الكسلان ينام نصف اليوم

Sloths sleep for at least half the day.

الدببة تنام في الشتاء

Bears sleep all winter.

الحلزون ينام لسنوات!

Snails sleep for years!

الغوريلات تنام مثلنا

Gorillas sleep just like we do.

الأطفال تنام كثيرًا!

Babies sleep. A lot!

حتى الكبار و أخواننا و
أخواتنا الأكبر منا تنام

Even grown-ups and big brothers
and sisters sleep.

و انت؟
أنت ايضا تنام

And you?
You sleep too, of course.

تصبح على خير!

Good night!

Different Ways To Sleep

Diurnal - Active during the day and asleep at night. Humans are diurnal.

Nocturnal - Active at night and asleep during the day. Animals like bats and hedgehogs are nocturnal.

Crepuscular - Most active during dawn and dusk and sometimes on cloudy days and bright nights. Animals like bears and cats are crepuscular.

Metaturnal or Cathemeral - Active at various times during the day and night. Lions and rabbits are metaturnal. Some animals that switch from diurnal to nocturnal with the seasons are considered metaturnal.

طرق مختلفة للنوم

نهاري: نشيط في النهار و ينام في الليل, البشر و بعض الطيور نهاريين

ليلي: نشيط في الليل و ينام في النهار, الخفاش و القنفذ يعتبران من الحيوانات اليلية

شفقي: نشيط في الفجر او بعد غروب الشمس و ربما في الاجواء الغائمة او الليالي القمرية المضيئة, بعض الامثلة للحيوان الشفقي الدب و القطط

ميتاتيرنال: نشيط في بعض اوقات الليل و النهار, من هذه الحيوانات الاسود و الارانب تعتبر ميتاتيرنالية

Also Available in
English and Māori-English Editions

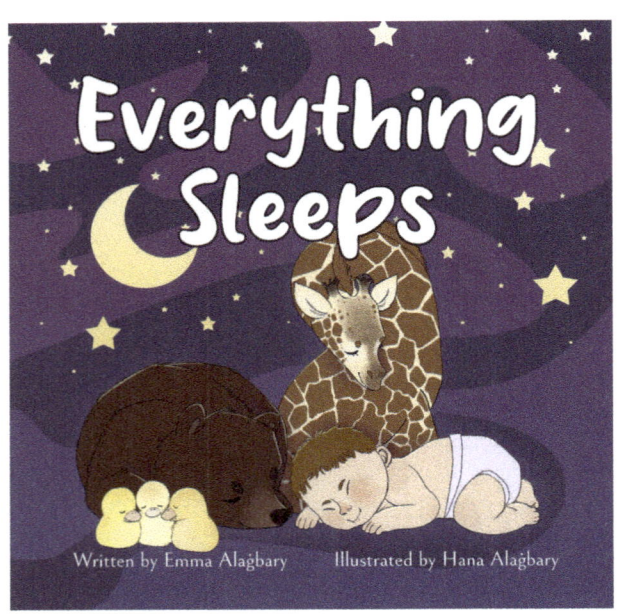
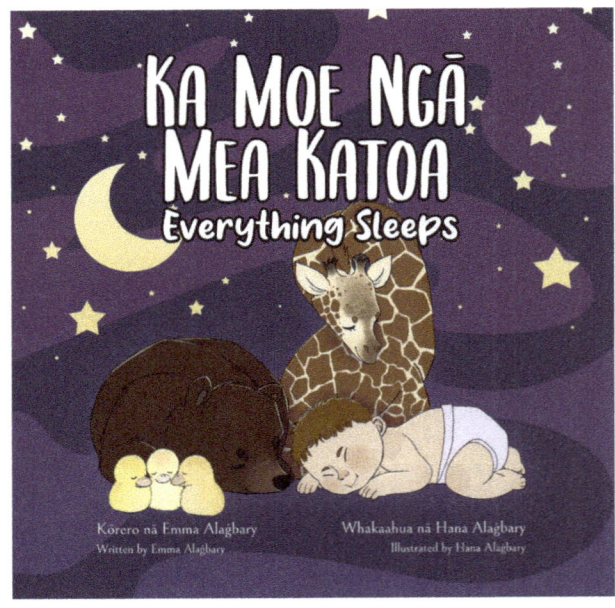

Little Dragon Books
treasures you can read

Did your children enjoy this book?

We're an independent publisher, support us by:
Leaving a review on Amazon and Goodreads.
Signing up to our newsletter littledragonbooks.com/news
Visiting our website and following our social media.
Asking your local library and bookstore to order our books.

littledragonbooks.com

www.ingramcontent.com/pod-product-compliance
Lightning Source LLC
Chambersburg PA
CBHW061800290426
44109CB00030B/2902